overneath

Copyright ©2003 Wendy Richmond

All rights reserved. No part of this book may be reproduced in any form by electronic or mechanical means (including photocopying, recording, or information storage and retrieval) without written permission from the author.

Funded in part by the LEF Foundation

Printed and bound in the United States of America

ISBN 0-9723026-0-3

www.wrichmond.com

Wendy Richmond

overneath

Contents

1   Plates

57 overneath

65 Snappy Dance Theater

67 Wendy Richmond

69 Acknowledgements

73 Colophon

10

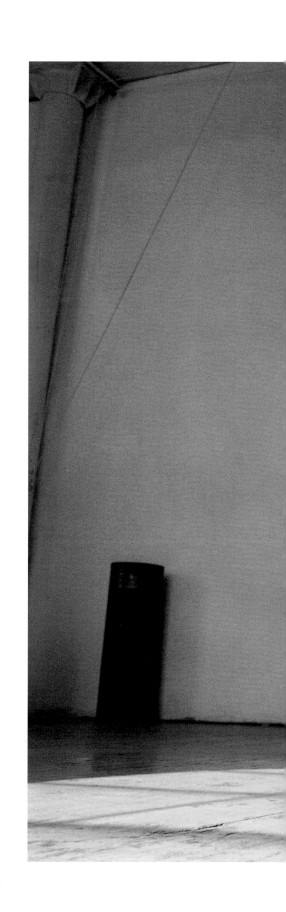

50

overneath

I ONCE ASKED A FRIEND how he would describe my work. He said, "You're a director of single frame movies."

I make photographs. I set up scenes in my studio using props that I have found or constructed, and I create a dialogue between these "characters." I stack, balance and suspend them so that they are precarious and dependent, exploring whatever activity or emotion they might suggest. I use the camera to find and record interactions that are intimate, ambiguous, and maybe absurd. I set it all up, and then look for something that I didn't expect.

When I first watched Snappy Dance Theater perform, it was like seeing my own artistic voice in another medium. I called Martha Mason, the artistic director of Snappy, and began sitting in on rehearsals. I watched the dancers as they improvised funny, strange and risky entanglements, alternating between control and letting go. Their process produced surprises, each one a building block for the next.

Soon after, I invited Martha to my studio. As we became familiar with each other's work and ideas, we decided to develop a collaboration. Our mutual ambition was clear: we wanted to push our respective work into unknown territory, to encourage risk and discovery by sharing and exchanging our creative tools and vocabulary.

Our collaboration has taken the form of process and product. The product has two independent components: a new dance work choreographed by Martha and a photographic series created by me. Our process is a sequence of physical dialogues between people, props, space and a camera.

MARTHA AND I WERE EAGER to learn from each other's practice and experience. Martha wanted to explore themes from an external factor to influence the choreography. I wanted to employ a deeper and more daring physicality in my image-making. We were also curious about using each other's tools. Martha had never used photography as an integral defining element of choreography. I had never used dancers as characters—performers who would work with me to explore and develop a series of interactions.

Our basic working premise was a process of ongoing dialogue. Over a six-month period, the dancers came to my studio and improvised movements, using props and set-ups from my previous installations. I photographed these movements, developed the film, and when the dancers returned for the next session, I showed them a selection of pictures. After absorbing and discussing the photographs, they continued to improvise.

During our improv/photography sessions, a process of repartee developed: the props influenced the movement, which then influenced the photography, which in turn influenced the movement, and so on. Each step along the way, whether it was spinning upside down or waiting for the right light, was part of our dialogue. Every movement, idea, and image spawned another. We were responding to each other and to each other's work.

It was also a dialogue in which we all familiarized ourselves with the aspects of a new and different medium. My work as a visual artist is typically about finding a series of discrete single moments; the dancers' work is about creating a flow of transitions. As a result of looking through each other's filters, the dancers became aware of constructed moments of stillness, and I began to find the action in between.

THE PROPS INCLUDED FIFTEEN rigid, metal-rimmed tubes that weighed approximately ten pounds each, with diameters ranging from ten to fourteen inches. Clothing was pedestrian, with sturdy shoes for comfort and safety; the floor was rough and the tubes were heavy. We met in the afternoon when the sunlight came through the west windows, moving across the floor and up the walls as the hours passed.

The dancers developed an almost literal attachment to the tubes. They became intimately familiar with each tube's personality: its weight, rustiness, the hardness of its metal rims, its bruises and signs of wear and age, even its individual beauty. In order to create and sustain movements, the dancers came to understand their counterparts in terms of their own bodies. Tubes, legs, arms and torsos were constantly shifting placement and roles: friend or adversary, support or burden, appendage or vessel.

When I asked the dancers to reflect on their movements, their descriptions included physical effort and visual metaphor. One dancer said, "I was on my back, with the tubes on my arms and legs pointing up, and at first I felt trapped. The weight was hard to hold up, and if one leg fell, the whole thing went down. Like a stiff-bodied dead bug turned on its side. But once I got the hang of it, the tubes would move pretty smoothly around, like a sea creature in the water's changing current. Sometimes, after wearing the tubes for a long time, I had to get my land legs back."

The company members of Snappy Dance Theater have wide and varied backgrounds. They are trained in ballet, modern dance, puppetry, gymnastics, theater, circus performance, and martial arts. They combined these talents with a curiosity, willingness and even a desire to spend hours hovering, balancing and back-bending on a wobbly circumference, or wearing multiple ten-pound tubes while groping at each other, blind except for a tiny view of the floor. In a matter of weeks, their bodies learned to accommodate these foreign objects as though they were natural extensions.

I tried the same moves myself and felt my awkwardness. I realized how difficult it is not only to have tubes as body parts, but also to have that many ideas for my body to express. When you are not a dancer or an actor, and you don't use your body as a vehicle for expression, you have a very limited vocabulary. You're inarticulate, and you may not even know if you have anything to say.

THE DANCERS BECAME my tools as well as my subject matter. They were constantly being watched, encouraged, framed, and captured by my camera and me.

Just as the dancers had to get used to being tools and growing new appendages, I had to get to know new characters. I was now working with foreign bodies in my studio. On one hand, I had more control: I had actual, live characters to whom I could relate my wishes and intentions. On the other hand, I could no longer dictate the scene. I began with a carefully chosen set of tools and expertise—sketches, dancers, space, light, clothing, tubes, film and lenses—and then I let go. Every element was constantly changing, depending on what the dancers were doing and what I was seeing. We were working through response, building on each other's moves, ideas, risks, and tumbles. Armed with my camera, I moved back, under, above, and in between. At times I felt like I was dancing.

WENDY RICHMOND
AUGUST 2002

SNAPPY DANCE THEATER

Founded in 1997, Snappy Dance Theater is a collaborative ensemble celebrating the varied movement backgrounds of its members. Athletics, gymnastics, circus skills, martial arts, vocal work, theater and dance are all incorporated in order to create works of diverse interest and appeal. Snappy takes its audience on an emotional journey that is humorous, thought provoking, and filled with surprises.

Martha Mason, Snappy Co-founder and Artistic Director, says, "I am most intrigued with work that is ambiguous in its tone—a situation that appears humorous suddenly becomes stunningly beautiful, or a grotesque character becomes clown-like. My role as the artistic director is to guide the company members in a direction that reflects the voice of Snappy and to simultaneously encourage individual movement and theater backgrounds. My process with Snappy has always been to allow initial time for play, to get everyone's creative juices flowing in a non-pressure environment and then find those moments within the dancers' improvisations that excite me the most."

www.snappydance.com

MARTHA MASON, CO-FOUNDER AND ARTISTIC DIRECTOR

Martha Mason, Co-founder and Artistic Director of Snappy Dance Theater, has been dancing for 28 years. She has received a NEFA "New Forms" award, two International Theatre Institute awards and two LEF New England grants, among others. She has performed, choreographed and taught in Europe, Russia, Taiwan and New York City and Boston.

THE COMPANY:
Jim Banta
Cathy Bosch
Bonnie Duncan
Sean Kilbridge
Bess Whitesel

WENDY RICHMOND

Wendy Richmond is the recipient of a Rockefeller Foundation residency in Bellagio, Italy, a LEF Foundation grant, a National Endowment for the Arts grant, and numerous art and design awards. Her installations and photographs have been exhibited in the United States and Europe. Richmond is the author of *Design & Technology: Erasing the Boundaries*, published by Van Nostrand Reinhold. Her regular column, in which she explores creativity in visual media, has appeared in *Communication Arts* magazine since 1983. She was co-founder and co-director of the Design Lab at WGBH TV, and has served on the AIGA National Board of Directors. She has taught at the School of the Museum of Fine Arts, Northeastern University and Harvard University. Richmond is currently Lecturer on Education at Harvard Graduate School of Education, where she has been teaching since 1996.

www.wrichmond.com

ACKNOWLEDGEMENTS

My collaboration with Martha Mason came from the most simple impetus: we wanted to work together. I am deeply grateful for her talent, intelligence, vision and friendship.

Martha and I are both grateful to the LEF Foundation for their generous support.

My energetic thanks go to Snappy Dance Theater company members, each of whom was a constant source of inspiration: Jim Banta, Cathy Bosch, Bonnie Duncan, Sean Kilbridge and Bess Whitesel.

I am most fortunate to have friends, colleagues and family who are enormously insightful and supportive, and who are also generous with their expertise and advice. My gratitude goes to my family and to Ronn Campisi, Joseph Carroll, Susan Hodara, Randy Garber, Richard Grossman, Alicia Staples, Jurgen Weiss, and above all and overneath to my husband Fred Raab.

COLOPHON

Printed by The Stinehour Press, Lunenburg, VT

Stock is Centura 100# text and Centura 120# cover

Type is Hoefler Text and Titling

Photographs shot with Scala film

Design by Wendy Richmond

Typography and production by Alicia Staples